This Journal
Belongs to

_____

Written and compiled by Marjorie Vawter.

ISBN 978-1-64352-153-4

Published by Barbour Books, an imprint of Barbour Publishing, Inc., 1810 Barbour Drive, Uhrichsville, Ohio 44683, www.barbourbooks.com

Our mission is to inspire the world with the life-changing message of the Bible.

Member of the
Evangelical Christian
Publishers Association

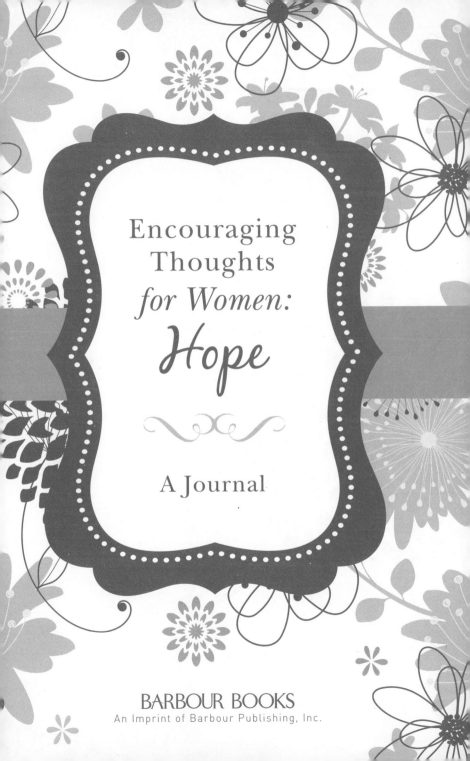

Encouraging Thoughts
for Women:
Hope

A Journal

BARBOUR BOOKS
An Imprint of Barbour Publishing, Inc.

Contents

Introduction

Faith shows the reality of what we hope for;
it is the evidence of things we cannot see.

HEBREWS 11:1 NLT

. . . .

We often use the word *hope* as a wish, wanting a certain outcome but uncertain it will happen that way. The actual definition of *hope* is a "desire accompanied by expectation of or belief in fulfillment." Not only is *hope* a longing for something we fully expect to happen—the anticipation of heaven for the believer, for example—but it is also an expectation that life has meaning and purpose, which is found only in Jesus Christ. Hope is a deep-down trust in our Abba Father that has roots from before the foundation of the world and extends into eternity. It is trust, confidence, dependence, faith, refuge, expectation, and strength all wrapped into one word—*hope.* May your hope be strengthened as you read these pages.

Abundant Living

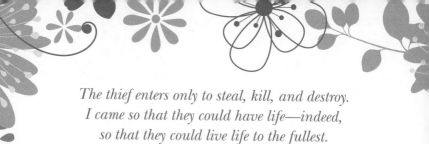

The thief enters only to steal, kill, and destroy.
I came so that they could have life—indeed,
so that they could live life to the fullest.
JOHN 10:10 CEB

Several times in Jesus' earthly ministry, He used examples from everyday life in first-century Israel to teach a spiritual truth. In John 10, He told the story of a shepherd coming to care for His flock. Jesus described a common practice of keeping the sheep within the household walls, so that the porter controlled who went in and out of the fold. Even if a stranger managed to get past the porter and into the pen with the sheep, they would ignore him. The sheep only have ears for their master's voice.

When the disciples didn't understand what Jesus wanted them to learn from the parable, He told it again in greater detail, in terms they could understand. The thief, Satan, only wants in the fold to steal, kill, and destroy. Jesus contrasted that with why He came. . . . So that every person could live a full, abundant life that doesn't end here on earth but continues on into eternity.

Jesus wasn't talking about material possessions but of His followers' spiritual life. He came to give us life—full, abundant, and free—forever. Like a well of water, it springs up within us and overflows onto those around us. Life with Jesus is more than we could ever imagine. And the abundance never, ever ends.

I pray that God, the source of hope, will fill you completely with joy and peace because you trust in him. Then you will overflow with confident hope through the power of the Holy Spirit.

ROMANS 15:13 NLT

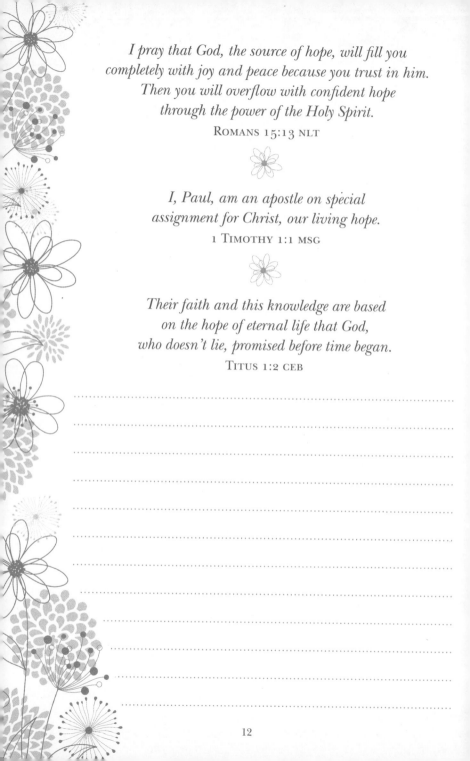

I, Paul, am an apostle on special assignment for Christ, our living hope.

1 TIMOTHY 1:1 MSG

Their faith and this knowledge are based on the hope of eternal life that God, who doesn't lie, promised before time began.

TITUS 1:2 CEB

Man can live about forty days without food, about
three days without water, about eight minutes without air,
but only for one second without hope.

HAL LINDSEY

Strong hope is a much greater stimulant
of life than any realized joy could be.

FRIEDRICH NIETZSCHE

Of all the forces that make for a better world,
none is so indispensable, none so powerful, as hope.
Without hope people are only half alive.
With hope they dream and think and work.

CHARLES SAWYER

Dancing in the Puddles

And so, Lord, where do I put my hope? My only hope is in you.
PSALM 39:7 NLT

They say you can tell a lot about a person's foundation of hope by the way she handles a rainy day. Does she turn into a gloomy Gussy, wailing, "Oh, woe is me. . ." or does she make the best of a bad situation? A hope-filled person will realize that abundant life in Christ isn't about simply enduring the storm but also about learning to dance in the puddles. So grab your galoshes, and let's boogie!

Source of Hope

Father God, You are our source of hope. Because of Jesus, we can expect to live full, satisfying lives, not only here on earth but also for eternity in heaven. Fill us to overflowing with Your joy and peace because of the confident hope we have through Your indwelling Holy Spirit. May this hope draw those around us to faith and hope in You. In Jesus' name, amen.

....

....

....

....

....

....

....

....

....

....

....

....

....

....

....

....

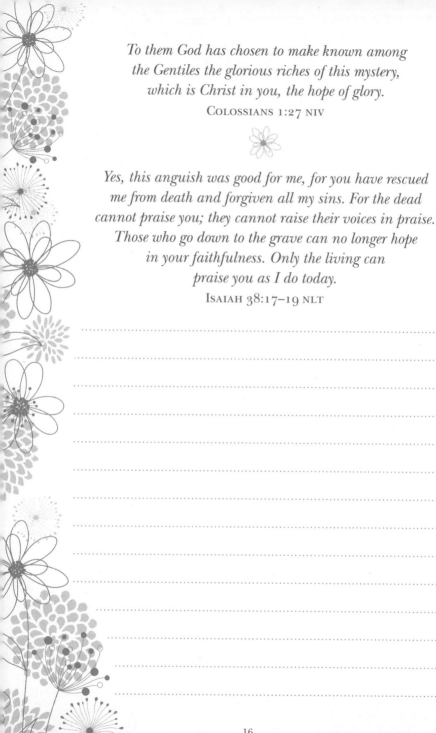

*To them God has chosen to make known among
the Gentiles the glorious riches of this mystery,
which is Christ in you, the hope of glory.*

COLOSSIANS 1:27 NIV

*Yes, this anguish was good for me, for you have rescued
me from death and forgiven all my sins. For the dead
cannot praise you; they cannot raise their voices in praise.
Those who go down to the grave can no longer hope
in your faithfulness. Only the living can
praise you as I do today.*

ISAIAH 38:17–19 NLT

The life of the godly is full of light and joy,
but the light of the wicked will be snuffed out.

May the God and Father of our Lord Jesus Christ be blessed!
On account of his vast mercy, he has given us new birth.
You have been born anew into a living hope through
the resurrection of Jesus Christ from the dead.

"A thief is only there to steal and kill and destroy.
I [Jesus] came so they can have real and eternal life,
more and better life than they ever dreamed of."

Shouts of Joy

He will yet fill your mouth with laughter
and your lips with shouts of joy.
JOB 8:21 NIV

Do you remember the last time you laughed till you cried? For many of us, it's been far too long. Stress tends to steal our joy, leaving us humorless and oh-so-serious. But lightness and fun haven't disappeared forever. They may be buried beneath the snow of a long, wintery life season, but spring is coming, girls. Laughter will bloom again, and our hearts will soar as our lips shout with joy. Grasp that hope!

Laughter, the Best Medicine

Gracious Father, we thank You for the gifts of hope and laughter. Too often we allow the struggles and sorrows of life to steal the hope that lies within us. Jesus said He came to bring us life—a life that abounds in hope. A life that is more than we could ever dream or imagine outside of Him. A life that overflows to those who need Your hope and peace. Amen.

You are not here merely to make a living. You are here in order to enable the world to live more amply, with greater vision, with a finer spirit of hope and achievement. You are here to enrich the world, and you impoverish yourself if you forget the errand.

WOODROW T. WILSON

Where there's life, there's hope.

TERENCE

....

....

....

....

....

....

....

....

....

....

....

....

....

....

Confidence

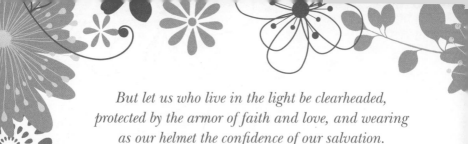

But let us who live in the light be clearheaded,
protected by the armor of faith and love, and wearing
as our helmet the confidence of our salvation.

1 THESSALONIANS 5:8 NLT

When David took on Goliath's challenge to fight to the death, King Saul attempted to dress the young shepherd in his adult-sized armor. Notice Saul didn't attempt to stop David, but he refused to send him out without more protection than David's everyday clothing. After he tried the armor, David took it off, saying he hadn't tested it (1 Samuel 17). Saul's armor would only hamper David rather than help. He was comfortable and confident in his own clothes.

On the cross Jesus paid the only price God would accept to cover our sins—His perfect lifeblood. The gift of salvation is free for all who will take it. At the same time God issues a full suit of armor to each of His children. He knows how fierce the battle can be against the enemy of our souls. And because the battle is fiercest in our minds, the helmet is key to protecting them.

Paul compared the helmet to ones worn by the Roman soldiers (Ephesians 6). This helmet was the warrior's most valuable, ornate, and expensive piece of equipment, complete with flaps that covered the cheeks, so it protected the entire head. When we accept Christ's payment on the cross for our sins, God gives us a similar helmet. All we have to do is put it on.

For I hope in You, O LORD; You will answer, O Lord my God.
PSALM 38:15 NASB

Why am I discouraged?
Why is my heart so sad?
I will put my hope in God!
I will praise him again—
my Savior and my God!
PSALM 42:11 NLT

For You are my hope; O Lord GOD,
You are my confidence from my youth.
PSALM 71:5 NASB

How blessed is he whose help is the God
of Jacob, whose hope is in the LORD his God.
PSALM 146:5 NASB

Optimism is the faith that leads to achievement.
Nothing can be done without hope and confidence.
HELEN KELLER

You are as young as your faith, as old as your doubt;
as young as your self-confidence, as old as your fear;
as young as your hope, as old as your despair.
SAMUEL ULLMAN

History informs us of past mistakes from which we can
learn without repeating them. It also inspires us and gives
confidence and hope bred of victories already won.
WILLIAM HASTIE

....

....

....

....

....

....

....

....

....

....

....

....

Getting to Know You

*For the law never made anything perfect. But now we have
confidence in a better hope, through which we draw near to God.*
HEBREWS 7:19 NLT

Following Old Testament law used to be considered the way to achieve
righteousness, but obeying rules just doesn't work for fallible humans.
We mess up. We fail miserably. Then Jesus came and provided a
better way to draw near to God. He bridged the gap by offering us a
personal relationship rather than rules. Together we laugh, cry, love,
grieve, rejoice. We get to know our Papa God through our personal
relationship with Him.

Praise Him

Father, we are so easily discouraged by events and circumstances we cannot control. They touch on emotions and trigger symptoms of depression and anxiety within us. It seems as though no one desires to seek You and Your solutions to the problems we face. But when we do look to You and seek to praise You in spite of our circumstances, Your hope infuses our souls and minds. And we cannot help but praise You. Amen.

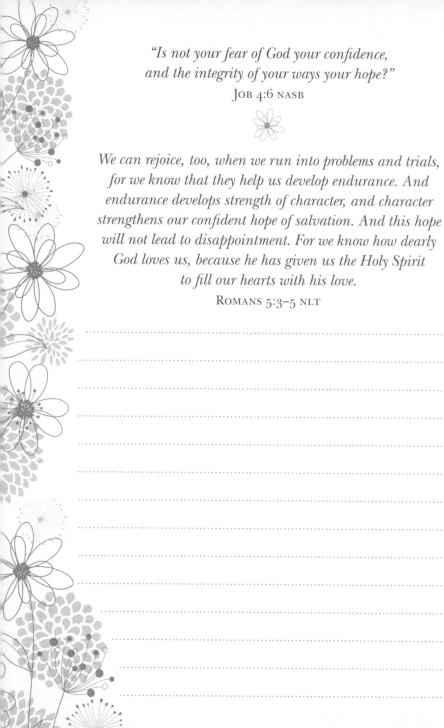

*"Is not your fear of God your confidence,
and the integrity of your ways your hope?"*
JOB 4:6 NASB

*We can rejoice, too, when we run into problems and trials,
for we know that they help us develop endurance. And
endurance develops strength of character, and character
strengthens our confident hope of salvation. And this hope
will not lead to disappointment. For we know how dearly
God loves us, because he has given us the Holy Spirit
to fill our hearts with his love.*
ROMANS 5:3–5 NLT

For the law never made anything perfect.
But now we have confidence in a better hope,
through which we draw near to God.

HEBREWS 7:19 NLT

I pray that your hearts will be flooded with light so that you can
understand the confident hope he has given to those he called—
his holy people who are his rich and glorious inheritance.

EPHESIANS 1:18 NLT

Smiling in the Darkness

The hopes of the godless evaporate.
JOB 8:13 NLT

Hope isn't just an emotion; it's a perspective, a discipline, a way of life. It's a journey of choice. We must learn to override those messages of discouragement, despair, and fear that assault us in times of trouble and press toward the light. Hope is smiling in the darkness. It's confidence that faith in God's sovereignty amounts to something. . . something life-changing, life-saving, and eternal.

Abba Father

Lord, because of Christ's work on the cross we are restored to fellowship with You. Our bodies are the temple where Your Holy Spirit lives. And the hope and confidence He brings with Him gives us the courage to persevere in the path You have laid out before us. You are our Abba Father, and as a child confident of her father's love is not shy to climb into his lap and make her request of his beneficence, neither should we be. Amen.

Morale is the state of mind. It is steadfastness and courage and hope. It is confidence and zeal and loyalty. It is élan, esprit de corps, and determination.

General George Catlett Marshall

He who has faith has. . .an inward reservoir of courage, hope, confidence, calmness, and assuring trust that all will come out well—even though to the world it may appear to come out most badly.

B. C. Forbes

Jesus, my Strength, my Hope, On Thee I cast my care, With humble confidence look up, And know Thou hear'st my prayer.

Charles Wesley

Courage

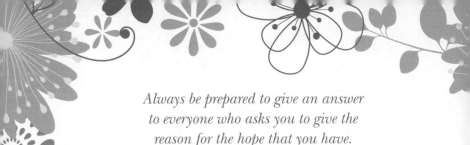

Always be prepared to give an answer
to everyone who asks you to give the
reason for the hope that you have.
But do this with gentleness and respect.
1 PETER 3:15 NIV

"What makes you people different from everyone else in this unit?" a nurse asked the young husband as she tended to the critical needs of his wife.

For the past several weeks, his wife had fought off infection, disease, and the partial shutdown of several of her organs while waiting for a liver transplant. Several times the doctors had given up, thinking she would die before the night was over. But the call for prayer went out over social media, and people all over the world prayed for this young couple.

Because she'd been a patient in the medical intensive care unit for over two months, the staff had had ample time to observe her and the family as they passed through crisis after crisis without complaint, without railing against those who were trying to help with little success, without blaming God.

Having had lots of time for thinking, praying, and reading God's Word, the young man was prepared for the question when it came. His wife belonged to God wholly and completely. It was their deep-down desire that God would get the glory no matter what happened. And because of their faith in Jesus Christ and their hope of eternal life after this life, they were able to face this deep trial of their faith with peace and a strength that came from the Lord.

Having hope will give you courage.
You will be protected
and will rest in safety.
JOB 11:18 NLT

So be strong and courageous,
all you who put your hope in the LORD!
PSALM 31:24 NLT

The high and lofty one who lives in eternity,
the Holy One, says this: "I live in the high and
holy place with those whose spirits are contrite and
humble. I restore the crushed spirit of the humble
and revive the courage of those with repentant hearts."
ISAIAH 57:15 NLT

Wait for the LORD; be strong
and let your heart take courage;
yes, wait for the LORD.
PSALM 27:14 NASB

There is hope in dreams, imagination, and in the courage
of those who wish to make those dreams a reality.

JONAS SALK

The stories of past courage can define that ingredient—
they can teach, they can offer hope, they can provide
inspiration. But they cannot supply courage itself.
For this each man must look into his own soul.

JOHN F. KENNEDY

If you lose hope, somehow you lose the vitality that
keeps life moving, you lose that courage to be,
that quality that helps you go on in spite of it all.

MARTIN LUTHER KING JR.

Bigger than Fear

Having hope will give you courage.
You will be protected and will rest in safety.
JOB 11:18 NLT

Tossing, turning, sleepless nights: What woman doesn't know these intimately? Our thoughts race with the "what ifs" and fear steals our peace. How precious is God's promise that He will rescue us from nagging, faceless fear and give us courage to just say no to anxious thoughts that threaten to terrorize us at our most vulnerable moments. He is our hope and protector. He is bigger than fear. Anxiety flees in His presence. Rest with Him tonight.

Facing Fear

Father, Your Word says You are always with us, even in the Valley of the Shadow of Death. Our hope in Jesus Christ gives us courage to face the darkest trials. Your peace dispels fear of the unknown and calms our spirits to hear your comforting voice giving us direction and clarity in decision-making and in speaking to others of Your love, grace, and mercy. Thank You. In Jesus' name, amen.

I eagerly expect and hope that I will in no way be ashamed, but will have sufficient courage so that now as always Christ will be exalted in my body, whether by life or by death.
PHILIPPIANS 1:20 NIV

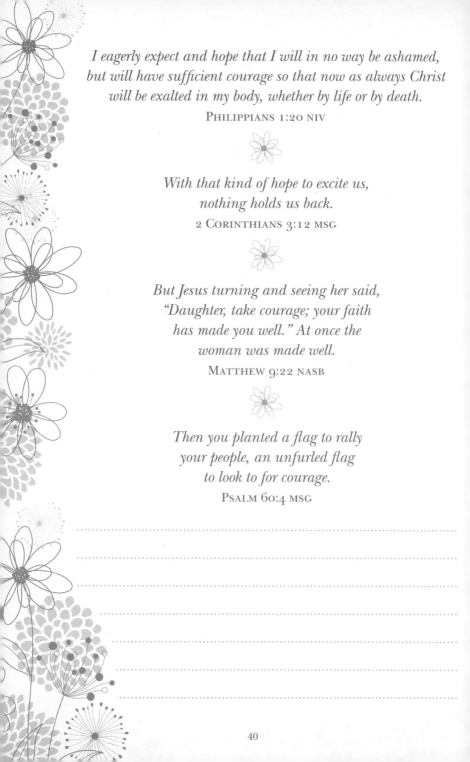

With that kind of hope to excite us, nothing holds us back.
2 CORINTHIANS 3:12 MSG

But Jesus turning and seeing her said, "Daughter, take courage; your faith has made you well." At once the woman was made well.
MATTHEW 9:22 NASB

Then you planted a flag to rally your people, an unfurled flag to look to for courage.
PSALM 60:4 MSG

....
....
....
....
....
....
....

Tell fearful souls, "Courage! Take heart!
GOD is here, right here, on his way to put
things right and redress all wrongs.
He's on his way! He'll save you!"

ISAIAH 35:4 MSG

"Be strong. Take courage. Don't be intimidated. Don't
give them a second thought because GOD, your God,
is striding ahead of you. He's right there with you.
He won't let you down; he won't leave you."

DEUTERONOMY 31:6 MSG

"Will your courage endure or your hands be
strong in the day I deal with you? I the
LORD have spoken, and I will do it."

EZEKIEL 22:14 NIV

....
....
....
....
....
....
....
....
....

No Wimps Here

*For God has not given us a spirit of fear and
timidity, but of power, love, and self-discipline.*
2 TIMOTHY 1:7 NLT

Do you suffer paralysis by analysis? Are you so afraid of trying
something new that you put it off until you can think it through. . .
and end up doing nothing at all? Too much introspection creates
inertia, and we abhor the ineffective wimps we become. Sisters, God
never intended for us to be wimps. His power and love are available
to replace our fear and infuse us with courage. Shake off that paralysis and get moving!

Facing Fear

Lord, it's so easy to allow fear to keep us from moving forward in life. Fear of an illness, fear of how others perceive us, fear of something new, fear of the unknown, fear of inadequacy. Help us remember that courage isn't the absence of fear; it's pressing on in spite of it. It helps to know You are right beside us, reminding us that Your perfect love casts out fear. Keep our eyes on Jesus today.

Courage is like love; it must have
hope to nourish it.

SAINT NAPOLEON BONAPARTE

Hope has two beautiful daughters; their names are
anger and courage. Anger that things are the way they
are. Courage to make them the way they ought to be.

SAINT AUGUSTINE

Whatever enlarges hope will also exalt courage.

SAMUEL JOHNSON

Woe is me if I do not preach the Gospel; if I did not aim
at that and possess faith and hope in Christ, it would be
bad for me indeed, but no, I have some courage.

VINCENT VAN GOGH

Future

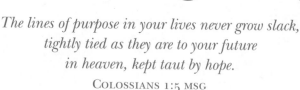

The lines of purpose in your lives never grow slack,
tightly tied as they are to your future
in heaven, kept taut by hope.
COLOSSIANS 1:5 MSG

Have you ever wondered what God's purpose is for you, whether here on earth or in our future home in heaven? The apostle Paul, formerly known as Saul, knew exactly what God's purpose was for stopping him on the road to Damascus. Those three days after his encounter with Jesus must have been one intense conversation with his new Master. After all, Saul's life radically changed from "breathing threats and murder against the disciples of the Lord" to becoming "a chosen instrument" to bear Christ's name "before the Gentiles and kings and the sons of Israel" (Acts 9:1, 15 NASB). Even his name changed.

God has a plan, a purpose, for each one of us. It may not be as clear as it was for Paul, but we don't need to worry. The Lord will make it plain in His time. In the meantime, we can know that having the hope of salvation and eternal life in heaven is keeping those lines of purpose taut. He will never let us go; He will never let His purposes for us fade. As He told Israel in exile in Babylon, He also tells us today, "I know what I'm doing. I have it all planned out—plans to take care of you, not abandon you, plans to give you the future you hope for" (Jeremiah 29:11 MSG).

And we believers also groan, even though we have the Holy Spirit within us as a foretaste of future glory, for we long for our bodies to be released from sin and suffering. We, too, wait with eager hope for the day when God will give us our full rights as his adopted children, including the new bodies he has promised us. We were given this hope when we were saved.

ROMANS 8:23–24 NLT

Because of his grace he declared us righteous and gave us confidence that we will inherit eternal life.

TITUS 3:7 NLT

I don't know about tomorrow;
It may bring me poverty.
But the one who feeds the sparrow,
Is the one who stands by me.
And the path that is my portion
May be through the flame or flood;
But His presence goes before me
And I'm covered with His blood.
Many things about tomorrow
I don't seem to understand
But I know who holds tomorrow
And I know who holds my hand.

IRA FOREST STAMPHILL

Beyond the Horizon

*Always continue to fear the LORD.
You will be rewarded for this;
your hope will not be disappointed.*
PROVERBS 23:17–18 NLT

Have you ever traversed a long, winding road, unable to see your final destination? Perhaps you were surprised by twists and turns along the way or jarred by unexpected potholes. But you were confident that if you stayed on that road, you would eventually reach your destination. Likewise, God has mapped out our futures. The end of the road may disappear beyond the horizon, but we are assured that our destination will not be disappointing.

Tomorrow

Gracious Lord, we may not know about tomorrow, but we do know the One who does. Sometimes You allow us glimpses, but You desire that we learn to leave the future in Your hands. You know the pitfalls as well as the delights. Your presence goes before us, behind us, and beside us. Surround us with Your peace that passes all understanding as we travel the path You have ordained for us. Amen.

And if our hope in Christ is only for this life,
we are more to be pitied than anyone in the world.
1 CORINTHIANS 15:19 NLT

For there is one body and one Spirit, just as you
have been called to one glorious hope for the future.
EPHESIANS 4:4 NLT

We want you to know what will happen
to the believers who have died so you will
not grieve like people who have no hope.
1 THESSALONIANS 4:13 NLT

We wait for the blessed hope—the appearing of the
glory of our great God and Savior, Jesus Christ.
TITUS 2:13 NIV

....
....
....
....
....
....
....
....
....

If we already have something, we don't need to hope for it.
But if we look forward to something we don't yet have,
we must wait patiently and confidently.

ROMANS 8:24–25 NLT

Such things were written in the Scriptures long ago to teach
us. And the Scriptures give us hope and encouragement
as we wait patiently for God's promises to be fulfilled.

ROMANS 15:4 NLT

Keep yourselves in the love of God, waiting anxiously
for the mercy of our Lord Jesus Christ to eternal life.

JUDE 1:21 NASB

....

....

....

....

....

....

....

....

....

....

....

....

Keep Breathing, Sister!

As long as we are alive, we still have hope,
just as a live dog is better off than a dead lion.
ECCLESIASTES 9:4 CEV

Isn't this a tremendous scripture? At first glance, the ending elicits a chuckle. But consider the truth it contains: Regardless of how powerful, regal, or intimidating a lion is, when he's dead, he's dead. But the living—you and I—still have hope. Limitless possibilities! Hope for today and for the future. Although we may be as lowly dogs, fresh, juicy bones abound. As long as we're breathing, it's not too late!

End Times

Father, how we long for the soon return of Your Son, Jesus Christ! He said that as it was in the days of Noah so it will be when He returns. Each day the world seems to grow worse; sin is more open and rampant, even acceptable. Our loved ones are taken from us. Fools and mockers are our leaders. But through it all we have the bright hope of heaven before us. Even so, come quickly, Lord Jesus. Amen.

Be still, my soul! thy God doth undertake
To guide the future as he has the past.
Thy hope, thy confidence let nothing shake;
All now mysterious shall be bright at last.
Be still, my soul! the waves and
winds still know His voice who
ruled them while He dwelt below.

KATHARINA VON SCHLEGEL

God's Faithful Love

Yet I still dare to hope when I remember this:
The faithful love of the LORD never ends!
His mercies never cease. Great is his faithfulness;
his mercies begin afresh each morning.
LAMENTATIONS 3:21–23 NLT

Jeremiah wrote the book of Lamentations after Nebuchadnezzar and his Babylonian army ransacked Jerusalem the final time. Only a remnant was left to live among the ruins of the temple and the city. Everyone else was either dead or on their way into exile in Babylon.

When God called Jeremiah to be His prophet and to preach warning after warning to Jeremiah's spiritually deaf countrymen, He told him that no one would listen to him. And no one did. Persecuted for his message, he was put in an old cistern in an attempt to silence him. His scribe, Baruch, faithfully wrote down the messages Jeremiah preached—only to have the king's men confiscate it and burn it at the king's orders. Baruch rewrote. And still no one listened.

The first twenty verses in Lamentations 3 are super depressing to read. But then, in verses 22 and 23, Jeremiah remembered a principle that caused his hope to burst forth anew: "The faithful love of the LORD never ends! His mercies never cease. Great is his faithfulness; his mercies begin afresh each morning" (NLT).

God's mercies and faithfulness are still available to His people today, many centuries later. They are still fresh every morning. In the direst of circumstances we have hope that one day it will be better. Great is His faithfulness.

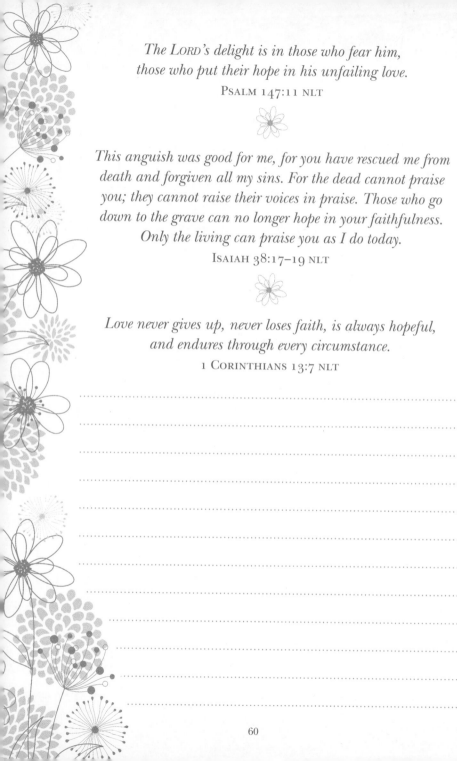

The LORD's delight is in those who fear him,
those who put their hope in his unfailing love.
PSALM 147:11 NLT

This anguish was good for me, for you have rescued me from
death and forgiven all my sins. For the dead cannot praise
you; they cannot raise their voices in praise. Those who go
down to the grave can no longer hope in your faithfulness.
Only the living can praise you as I do today.
ISAIAH 38:17–19 NLT

Love never gives up, never loses faith, is always hopeful,
and endures through every circumstance.
1 CORINTHIANS 13:7 NLT

Lord, make me an instrument of your peace; where there is hatred, let me sow love; where there is injury, pardon; where there is doubt, faith; where there is despair, hope; where there is darkness, light; and where there is sadness, joy.

SAINT FRANCIS OF ASSISI

To love is to risk not being loved in return. To hope is to risk pain. To try is to risk failure, but risk must be taken because the greatest hazard in life is to risk nothing.

LEO BUSCAGLIA

Love, we say, is life; but love without hope and faith is agonizing death.

ELBERT HUBBARD

....
....
....
....
....
....
....
....
....
....
....
....

Everyday Blessings

But the eyes of the LORD are on those who fear him,
on those whose hope is in his unfailing love.

PSALM 33:18 NIV

The Lord of all creation is watching our every moment and wants to fill us with His joy. He often interrupts our lives with His blessings: butterflies dancing in sunbeams, dew-touched spiderwebs, cotton candy clouds, and glorious crimson sunsets. The beauty of His creation reassures us of His unfailing love and fills us with hope. But it is up to us to take the time to notice.

Love Never Fails

Loving Father, we praise You for the ultimate measure of Your love for us: You sent Your Son to die for our sins. How do we repay such a gift? We cannot. Yet in love and gratitude for Your generosity we can do nothing less than give You our best. You are the perfect example of unconditional love. May our lives reflect that to a lost and dying world. Amen.

Know therefore that the L<small>ORD</small> *your God is God; he is the faithful God, keeping his covenant of love to a thousand generations of those who love him and keep his commands.*

D<small>EUTERONOMY</small> 7:9 <small>NIV</small>

Your love, G<small>OD</small>, *is my song, and I'll sing it! I'm forever telling everyone how faithful you are.*

P<small>SALM</small> 89:1 <small>MSG</small>

Give thanks to the L<small>ORD</small>, *for he is good! His faithful love endures forever.*

1 C<small>HRONICLES</small> 16:34 <small>NLT</small>

Love the L<small>ORD</small>, *all you godly ones! For the* L<small>ORD</small> *protects those who are loyal to him, but he harshly punishes the arrogant.*

P<small>SALM</small> 31:23 <small>NLT</small>

*[Nehemiah] said: "LORD God of heaven, great and awesome
God, you are the one who keeps covenant and is truly faithful
to those who love you and keep your commandments."*

NEHEMIAH 1:5 CEB

*His love has taken over our lives; GOD's
faithful ways are eternal. Hallelujah!*

PSALM 117:2 MSG

*Yes, goodness and faithful love will pursue
me all the days of my life, and I will live
in the LORD's house as long as I live.*

PSALM 23:6 CEB

....
....
....
....
....
....
....
....
....
....
....
....

I Do

Let us hold unswervingly to the hope we profess,
for he who promised is faithful.
HEBREWS 10:23 NIV

An important part of any marriage is the vow of faithfulness. We pledge that we will remain faithful to our beloved until death do us part. Faithfulness is crucial to a trusting relationship. We must be able to depend on our spouse to always be in our corner, love us even when we're unlovable, and never leave or forsake us. God is faithful. We can unswervingly depend on Him to never break His promises.

Faithful God

Father God, You are greatly to be praised for Your faithfulness to all generations. You are faithful in life, faithful in death, faithful in provision, faithful in strength, faithful in mercy, faithful in love. Every minute of every day Your faithfulness shines through. Open our eyes to see Your faithfulness in all You do. Every day Your mercies are new. Your grace is sufficient for each situation. We lift our arms in praise to You.

Our righteousness is in Him, and our hope depends,
not upon the exercise of grace in us, but upon the fullness of
grace and love in Him, and upon His obedience unto death.

JOHN NEWTON

They say a person needs just three things to
be truly happy in this world: someone to love,
something to do, and something to hope for.

TOM BODETT

Love's redeeming work is done, Alleluia!
Fought the fight, the battle won, Alleluia!
Death in vain forbids Him rise, Alleluia!
Christ hath opened paradise, Alleluia!

CHARLES WESLEY

God's Word

You are my refuge and my shield;
I have put my hope in your word.
PSALM 119:114 NIV

The shield used by the Roman soldiers was no small, light piece of protection. Many were the size of doors, big enough to stand behind and be completely sheltered from a barrage of fiery arrows or long spears. Made of wood, they were then covered with leather. Before battle, the soldiers would soak the entire shield with water, making them fire resistant. . .and heavier. These soldiers weren't wimps!

Because of the size of the shields, the Romans presented a formidable line when coming against a walled city. An entire unit would band together to form a tank-like barrier to the archers and other soldiers on the walls above them. The soldiers on the outside of the formation would place their shields vertically, making a solid wall around the unit. The soldiers in the center placed their shields above them horizontally, completely sealing the men within a fire-resistant box. This allowed them to get close to the walls to assault the gates or any weak areas at the foundations without a great sacrifice of lives.

This is the type of refuge we find in God's Word. When we put our hope in the promises God has laid out in His love letter to us, His Word surrounds us and protects us from the onslaught of fiery darts the enemy throws our way. What an awesome picture of God's provision for our safety in any circumstance.

....

....

....

....

Remember your promise to me; it is my only hope.
PSALM 119:49 NLT

May those who fear you rejoice when they see me,
for I have put my hope in your word.
PSALM 119:74 NIV

God can't break his word. And because his word cannot
change, the promise is likewise unchangeable. We who
have run for our very lives to God have every reason to
grab the promised hope with both hands and never let go.
HEBREWS 6:18 MSG

I am worn out waiting for your rescue,
but I have put my hope in your word.
PSALM 119:81 NLT

....

....

....

....

....

....

....

Waiting on God

Father, many times in the midst of a trial or battle, we find ourselves waiting on You. Waiting is hard, especially when we're surrounded by trouble and we need rescuing now. But the waiting is easier when You recall to our minds the promises of Your Word. Because You cannot lie, we can know You will come to our rescue, though it most likely will not be what we expect. Amen.

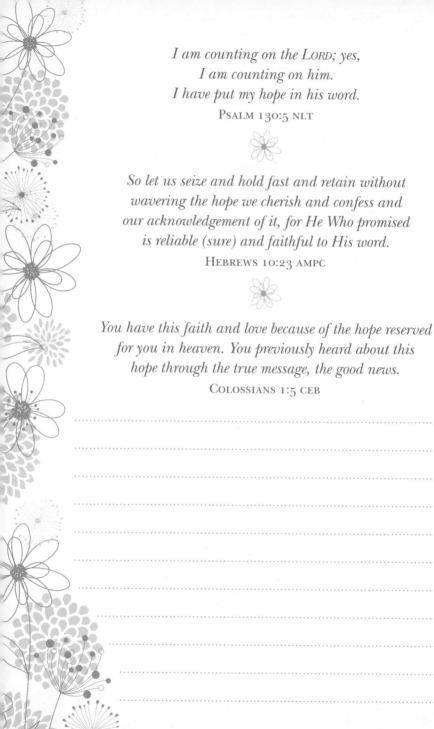

I am counting on the Lord; yes,
I am counting on him.
I have put my hope in his word.
PSALM 130:5 NLT

So let us seize and hold fast and retain without
wavering the hope we cherish and confess and
our acknowledgement of it, for He Who promised
is reliable (sure) and faithful to His word.
HEBREWS 10:23 AMPC

You have this faith and love because of the hope reserved
for you in heaven. You previously heard about this
hope through the true message, the good news.
COLOSSIANS 1:5 CEB

The Bible's words are our hope.

BILLY GRAHAM

Hope is the word which God has
written on the brow of every man.

VICTOR HUGO

Our Lord has written the promise of resurrection,
not in books alone, but in every leaf in springtime.

MARTIN LUTHER

The church's one foundation is Jesus Christ her Lord;
she is his new creation by water and the Word.
From heaven he came and sought her to be his holy bride;
with his own blood he bought her, and for her life he died.

SAMUEL J. STONE

....
....
....
....
....
....
....
....
....

Questions and Answers

*And the Scriptures were written to teach
and encourage us by giving us hope.*
ROMANS 15:4 CEV

What do you do when facing a perplexing problem? Ask a family member? Consult a friend? Turn to the Internet? God's Word is brimming with answers to life's difficulties, yet it's often the last place we turn. God speaks to us today through the lives of trusting Abraham, brokenhearted Ruth, runaway Jonah, courageous Esther, female leader Deborah in a male-dominated society, beaten-down Job, double-crossing Peter, and Paul, who proved people can change.

God Is Our Help

O God, so often the last place we turn to for help in times of trouble is where we should have gone in the first place. Give us such a thirst for Your Word that it saturates every part of our being, giving us relief sooner rather than later. Your Word is our meat and bread and contains the solutions to every problem. Thank You for this provision. We love You.

I was up before sunrise, crying for help,
hoping for a word from you.
PSALM 119:147 MSG

But if anyone obeys his word, love for God is truly made
complete in them. This is how we know we are in him.
1 JOHN 2:5 NIV

He that is of God heareth God's words.
JOHN 8:47 KJV

For the word of the LORD holds true,
and we can trust everything he does.
PSALM 33:4 NLT

I wait for God, my soul doth wait;
My hope is in His Word.
More than they that
for morning watch,
My soul waits for the Lord.

Scottish Psalter, 1650

The Word of God well understood and religiously
obeyed is the shortest route to spiritual perfection.
And we must not select a few favorite passages to
the exclusion of others. Nothing less than a whole
Bible can make a whole Christian.

A. W. Tozer

....

....

....

....

....

....

....

....

....

....

....

....

If You Build It, He Will Come

*Do not snatch your word of truth from me,
for your regulations are my only hope.*
PSALM 119:43 NLT

Bibles wear and tear. Papers get discarded. Hard drives crash. But memorizing scripture assures us that God's Word will never be lost. His truth will always be at our disposal, any moment of the day or night when we need a word of encouragement, of guidance, of hope. Like a phone call from heaven, our Father communicates to us via scripture implanted in our hearts. But it is up to us to build the signal tower.

Sin and God's Word

Father, many of us have a quote written in the fronts of our Bibles saying, "This Book will keep you from sin, or sin will keep you from this Book." What a great reminder to keep us in Your Word. Sharpen our minds so we can commit scripture to memory—another guard against sin when we recall it at a time of temptation. Teach us how to wield the Sword effectively. In Jesus' name, amen.

It does not require great learning to be
a Christian and be convinced of the truth
of the Bible. It requires only an honest
heart and a willingness to obey God.

ALBERT BARNES

All who call on God in true faith, earnestly from
the heart, will certainly be heard, and will
receive what they have asked and desired.

MARTIN LUTHER

The Bible is one of the greatest blessings bestowed
by God on the children of men. It has God for its
author, salvation for its end, and truth without
any mixture for its matter. It is all pure.

JOHN LOCKE

Joyful Living

*Be joyful in hope, patient in
affliction, faithful in prayer.*
ROMANS 12:12 NIV

Joyful in hope. Paul's letter to the Romans is a essay on salvation in Christ Jesus alone, written by a man who was skillfully trained in logic and the Law. The first five chapters describe how we are all condemned because of sin, how God provided the needed sacrifice to pay our debt to sin, and how that sacrifice satisfied the Law's demands. The next three chapters show how believers are molded and reshaped into the image of Christ. After reading and studying these chapters, it's difficult to suppress the joy resulting from the incredible hope we can find in Christ.

Patient in affliction. Paul's life is an example of patience in affliction. In his second letter to the Corinthians Paul lists the trials and difficulties he experienced since coming to know Christ as his Savior. "Labors. . .imprisonments. . .beaten. . .in danger of death. Five times. . .thirty-nine lashes. . .beaten with rods. . .I was stoned. . . shipwrecked," and many other dangers and trials (11:23–28 NASB). Are we willing to bear affliction for the cause of Christ?

Faithful in prayer. Paul's prayers are well documented in his letters to the churches. He pleaded with his readers to "pray at all times in the Spirit" (Ephesians 6:18), "pray without ceasing" (1 Thessalonians 5:17), and "to pray. . .without wrath and dissension" (1 Timothy 2:8). James tells us that "the effective prayer of a righteous man can accomplish much" (5:16). When we commit to pray for someone or for a situation, follow through. Prayer for one another strengthens not only the pray-er but also the entire body of believers.

I have set the Lord always before me: because he is at my right hand, I shall not be moved. Therefore my heart is glad, and my glory rejoiceth: my flesh also shall rest in hope.

PSALM 16:8–9 KJV

May the God of green hope fill you up with joy, fill you up with peace, so that your believing lives, filled with the life-giving energy of the Holy Spirit, will brim over with hope!

ROMANS 15:13 MSG

The hope of the righteous is gladness, but the expectation of the wicked perishes.

PROVERBS 10:28 NASB

....

....

....

....

....

....

....

....

....

....

Joy

Father, there's nothing like the deep-down joy imbedded deep within our souls. It is the undercurrent to life, running still and deep, never failing. Sometimes we bury it under the cares of life; other times it bubbles out in laughter and worship. It's more than being happy, though it is a close cousin to happiness. "Hope springs eternal" is true when it comes to the believer. What a glorious hope we have in Christ! Amen.

We put our hope in the LORD.
He is our help and our shield.
In him our hearts rejoice, for we
trust in his holy name. Let your
unfailing love surround us, LORD,
for our hope is in you alone.
PSALM 33:20–22 NLT

For who is our hope or joy
or crown of exultation?
Is it not even you,
in the presence of our
Lord Jesus at His coming?
1 THESSALONIANS 2:19 NASB

No wonder my heart is glad,
and my tongue shouts his praises!
My body rests in hope.
ACTS 2:26 NLT

Come, Thou long expected Jesus
Born to set Thy people free;
From our fears and sins release us,
Let us find our rest in Thee.
Israel's Strength and Consolation,
Hope of all the earth Thou art;
Dear Desire of every nation,
Joy of every longing heart.

CHARLES WESLEY

A propensity to hope and joy is real riches;
one to fear and sorrow real poverty.

DAVID HUME

Rejoice in glorious hope!
Jesus the Judge shall come,
And take His servants up
to their eternal home.

CHARLES WESLEY

Pick Me Up, Daddy

We boast in the hope of the glory of God.
ROMANS 5:2 NIV

To rejoice means to live joyfully…joy-fully…full of joy. Joy is a decision we make. A choice not to keep wallowing in the mud of our lives. And there will be mud—at one time or another. When spiritual rain mixes with the dirt of fallen people, mud is the inevitable result. The Creator of sparkling sunbeams, soaring eagles, and spectacular fuchsia sunsets wants to lift us out of the mud. Why don't we raise our arms to Him today?

Hope in Christ

Father God, we look forward to the hope of Christ's coming again. What a comfort and joy it is to know we will be reunited with our loved ones in Christ someday. What a reunion we have to look forward to. Because of Christ's death and resurrection, the sting of Death is gone, replaced by the glorious hope of eternal life with You. We will never cease to praise You. Amen.

The LORD taketh pleasure in them that fear him,
in those that hope in his mercy.
PSALM 147:11 KJV

This is the day which the LORD has made;
Let us rejoice and be glad in it.
PSALM 118:24 NASB

Weeping may last for the night,
but a shout of joy comes
in the morning.
PSALM 30:5 NASB

....
....
....
....
....
....
....
....
....
....
....
....

The trouble with many men is that they have got
just enough religion to make them miserable.
If there is not joy in religion, you have got
a leak in your religion.
BILLY SUNDAY

Your joy comes from how you think,
the choices that we make in life.
JOYCE MEYER

We have within ourselves
Enough to fill the present day with joy,
And overspread the future years with hope.
WILLIAM WORDSWORTH

....
....
....
....
....
....
....
....
....
....
....

Soul Sister

I always see the Lord near me, and I will not be afraid with him at my right side. Because of this, my heart will be glad, my words will be joyful, and I will live in hope.
ACTS 2:25–26 CEV

Laughter is the soul sister of joy; they often travel together. Humor is the primary catalyst for releasing joy into our souls and making our hearts glad. It's healthy for us too! Laughter is cleansing and healing, a powerful salve for the wounds of life. . .a natural medicine and tremendous stress reliever. Laughing is to joy what a 50% Off sign is to shopping. It motivates us to seek more, more, more!

A Living Hope

"O God, our help in ages past, our hope for years to come." How we praise You for the hope that sustains life in us. Even when earthly hopes disappoint and fail us, You are always with us, teaching us that true hope is found only in Jesus Christ, the hope of glory. This hope is alive, vibrant, and eternal. All praise and glory belong to You. Amen.

Hope is a state of mind, not of the world. Hope, in
this deep and powerful sense, is not the same as joy
that things are going well, or willingness to invest in
enterprises that are obviously heading for success, but
rather an ability to work for something because it is good.

VACLAV HAVEL

My spirits were elevated by the enchanting appearance
of nature; the past was blotted from my memory,
the present was tranquil, and the future gilded by
bright rays of hope and anticipations of joy.

MARY WOLLSTONECRAFT SHELLEY

Perseverance

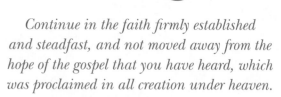

Continue in the faith firmly established
and steadfast, and not moved away from the
hope of the gospel that you have heard, which
was proclaimed in all creation under heaven.

COLOSSIANS 1:23 NASB

During a recent storm with high winds, several trees were uprooted, damaging homes, outbuildings, and vehicles and taking down power lines, knocking out electricity in the process of their fall. On the surface, the trees looked strong. But when the strong winds came, their roots were too shallow to hold the trees up.

Twice in scripture we're given a picture of a steadfast person who has firmly grounded herself in the Word. She is compared to a tree planted by water that has its roots extended deep into the ground, not depending on the surface water alone. It is not easily uprooted during the storms and winds of life. Instead it thrives in times of drought, putting out new leaves each spring and bearing abundant fruit each season.

The person who embraces the hope of the Gospel spends time in the Word and in prayer, stands firm in the storms, and will not give in to the winds that threaten to uproot it. Instead she digs her roots further into the ground and concentrates on producing fruit. Paul encouraged the Colossians to be mighty-tree believers in spite of the winds of persecution that threatened the very life of the early church. We too should be strong, gaining strength in the Gospel, nurturing our souls, and nourishing others.

But as for me, I will hope continually,
and will praise You yet more and more.
PSALM 71:14 NASB

When everything was hopeless, Abraham
believed anyway, deciding to live not on
the basis of what he saw he couldn't do but
on what God said he would do.
ROMANS 4:18 MSG

But Christ, as the Son, is in charge of God's entire house.
And we are God's house, if we keep our courage and
remain confident in our hope in Christ.
HEBREWS 3:6 NLT

....

....

....

....

....

....

....

....

....

....

Mighty Trees

Father, when the storms of life blow into our lives, we want to stand strong. But that doesn't happen quickly. We bend, and it seems we will break under the pressure life brings. Yet You have promised that those who spend time in Your Word and in prayer will be steadfast in the midst of trials. Make us like trees planted by the water, digging deep for nourishment, resting in Your strength. Amen.

We can rejoice, too, when we run into problems and trials, for we know that they help us develop endurance. And endurance develops strength of character, and character strengthens our confident hope of salvation. And this hope will not lead to disappointment. For we know how dearly God loves us, because he has given us the Holy Spirit to fill our hearts with his love.

ROMANS 5:3–5 NLT

*For his anger lasts only a moment,
but his favor lasts a lifetime; weeping may stay
for the night, but rejoicing comes in the morning.*

PSALM 30:5 NIV

Learn from yesterday, live for today, hope for tomorrow.
The important thing is not to stop questioning.
ALBERT EINSTEIN

Most of the important things in the world have been
accomplished by people who have kept on trying
when there seemed to be no hope at all.
DALE CARNEGIE

Hope begins in the dark, the stubborn hope that if you just
show up and try to do the right thing, the dawn will come.
You wait and watch and work; you don't give up.
ANNE LAMOTT

....

....

....

....

....

....

....

....

....

....

....

Nothing More Than Feelings

Lord, sustain me as you promised, that I may live!
Do not let my hope be crushed.

PSALM 119:116 NLT

Whatever our foe—unemployment, rejection, loss, illness—we may feel beaten down by life. Hope feels crushed by the relentless boulder bearing down on our souls. We think that we can't possibly endure another day. Yes, we feel, we feel. But feelings are often deceiving. God promises to sustain us, to strengthen us, so that we might withstand that massive rock. We can trust Him. He will not allow us to be crushed!

Fixed Hope

Lord, it seems so many believers waver in the face of criticism, intolerance, and persecution. How easy it is for us to take our eyes off the hope that is coming the hope of the revelation of Jesus Christ at His Second Coming, the hope of eternal life with You in heaven. The cares of life crowd out the time we used to spend with You. Restore hope. Prepare us for action. Amen.

Therefore, prepare your minds for action, keep sober in spirit, fix your hope completely on the grace to be brought to you at the revelation of Jesus Christ.

1 PETER 1:13 NASB

And our hope for you is firmly grounded, knowing that as you are sharers of our sufferings, so also you are sharers of our comfort.

2 CORINTHIANS 1:7 NASB

We remember before our God and Father your work produced by faith, your labor prompted by love, and your endurance inspired by hope in our Lord Jesus Christ.

1 THESSALONIANS 1:3 NIV

When I stand before God at the end of my life, I would
hope that I would not have a single bit of talent left,
and could say, "I used everything you gave me."
ERMA BOMBECK

In a mood of faith and hope my work goes on. A ream
of fresh paper lies on my desk waiting for the next book.
I am a writer and I take up my pen to write.
PEARL S. BUCK

Hope is the struggle of the soul, breaking loose from
what is perishable, and attesting her eternity.
HERMAN MELVILLE

Three things will last forever—
faith, hope, and love.
1 CORINTHIANS 13:13 NLT

Pay close attention to yourself and
to your teaching; persevere in these things,
for as you do this you will ensure salvation
both for yourself and for those who hear you.
1 TIMOTHY 4:16 NASB

Pursue righteousness, godliness, faith,
love, perseverance and gentleness.
1 TIMOTHY 6:11 NASB

Reliance

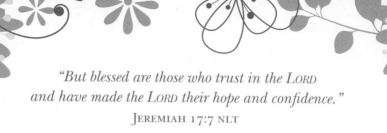

"I want you to go to my mountain and offer your son Isaac as a burnt offering to me."

When God spoke these words to Abraham, we're not told of his initial reaction to those words, or if there was one. In Genesis 22, the words immediately following God's command are "So, Abraham [obeyed]." He followed God's instructions to the letter. Even when Isaac questioned his father about the lack of a sacrifice, Abraham's only answer was "God will provide Himself an offering." And God did. But not until Abraham had tied up his son, laid him on the altar, and had the knife held high ready to plunge it into the son of promise.

What amazing faith! But it didn't happen overnight. Abraham's faith grew strong over many years of hearing God command and obeying without hesitation. The writer of Hebrews tells us, "Abraham figured that if God wanted to, he could raise the dead. In a sense, that's what happened when he received Isaac back, alive from off the altar" (11:19 MSG). God had already given them Isaac when Sarah's body was long past the age of childbearing. Abraham believed God when He first told Him he would be the father of many nations, and God counted it as righteousness. And God fulfilled His promise to Abraham, blessing him many times over for his implicit reliance on God.

*But the eyes of the LORD are on those
who fear him, on those whose hope
is in his unfailing love.*

PSALM 33:18 NIV

*Yet you brought me out of the womb; you made
me trust in you, even at my mother's breast.*

PSALM 22:9 NIV

*Through Christ you have come to trust in God. And you
have placed your faith and hope in God because he raised
Christ from the dead and gave him great glory.*

1 PETER 1:21 NLT

For thou art my hope, O Lord GOD:
thou art my trust from my youth.
PSALM 71:5 KJV

To hope means to be ready at every moment for that
which is not yet born, and yet not become desperate
if there is no birth in our lifetime.
ERICH FROMM

I'm possessed of a hope
that is steadfast and sure,
Since Jesus came into my heart!
And no dark clouds of doubt
now my pathway obscure,
Since Jesus came into my heart!
RUFUS H. MCDANIEL

....

....

....

....

....

....

....

....

....

Climb In

Trust is the bottom line when it comes to living an abundant life. We will never escape the muddy ruts without trusting that God has the leverage and power to pull us out of the quagmire. They say faith is like believing the tightrope walker can cross the gorge pushing a wheelbarrow. Trust is climbing into his wheelbarrow. Only when we climb into God's wheelbarrow can His joy and peace overflow as hope into our hearts.

Implicit Faith

Father, You are wholly trustworthy. Reading through the Hall of Faith in Hebrews 11 reinforces that truth. There is no reason to doubt Your goodness or purposes when You ask us to do something that makes no sense to our human minds. You promise great blessing for those who trust You wholly, one of which is filling us with hope in Christ Jesus. You are greatly to be praised. Amen.

O my God, I trust, lean on, rely on, and am confident
in You. Let me not be put to shame or [my hope in You]
be disappointed; let not my enemies triumph over me.
PSALM 25:2 AMPC

We put our hope in the LORD. He is our help
and our shield. In him our hearts rejoice, for we
trust in his holy name. Let your unfailing love
surround us, LORD, for our hope is in you alone.
PSALM 33:20–22 NLT

O God. . .You. . .are the confidence and hope of all
the ends of the earth and of those far off on the seas.
PSALM 65:5 AMPC

Those who trust in, lean on, and confidently hope in the Lord are like Mount Zion, which cannot be moved but abides and stands fast forever.
PSALM 125:1 AMPC

For the law never made anything perfect. But now we have confidence in a better hope, through which we draw near to God.
HEBREWS 7:19 NLT

So trust in the Lord (commit yourself to Him, lean on Him, hope confidently in Him) forever; for the Lord God is an everlasting Rock [the Rock of Ages].
ISAIAH 26:4 AMPC

True Success

"For I know the plans I have for you," declares the LORD,
"plans to prosper you and not to harm you,
plans to give you hope and a future."

JEREMIAH 29:11 NIV

As little girls, we dream about the handsome man we'll one day marry, exciting trips we'll take, the mansion we'll call home, and the beautiful, perfect children we'll have. A successful life—isn't that what we hope for? But God doesn't call us to be successful; He calls us to trust Him. We may never be successful in the world's eyes, but trust in our Father's omnipotence ensures our future and our hope. And that's true success.

No Matter What

Lord God, we desire the faith of those women of God who have gone before us. Sarah, the mother of Isaac; Deborah, the judge; Hannah who prayed for a son and then dedicated him to You; Mary, the mother of Jesus; Esther, the Persian queen who saved her nation from Haman's schemes; and so many more. No matter what, faith in You is much more satisfying than relying on ourselves. We love You.

[I do it because, though He slay me, yet will I wait for and trust Him and] behold, He will slay me; I have no hope—nevertheless, I will maintain and argue my ways before Him and even to His face.

JOB 13:15 AMPC

I pray that God, the source of hope, will fill you completely with joy and peace because you trust in him. Then you will overflow with confident hope through the power of the Holy Spirit.

ROMANS 15:13 NLT

And again He says, My trust and assured reliance and confident hope shall be fixed in Him.

HEBREWS 2:13 AMPC

I believe the single most significant decision I can make on a day-to-day basis is my choice of attitude. It is more important than my past, my education, my bankroll, my successes or failures, fame or pain, what other people think of me or say about me, my circumstances, or my position. Attitude keeps me going or cripples my progress. It alone fuels my fire or assaults my hope. When my attitudes are right, there is no barrier too high, no valley too deep, no dream too extreme, no challenge too great for me.

CHARLES R. SWINDOLL

God can't break his word. And because his word cannot change, the promise is likewise unchangeable. We who have run for our very lives to God have every reason to grab the promised hope with both hands and never let go. It's an unbreakable spiritual lifeline, reaching past all appearances right to the very presence of God.

HEBREWS 6:18–19 MSG

For we. . .by faith anticipate and wait for the blessing and good for which our righteousness and right standing with God [our conformity to His will in purpose, thought, and action, causes us] to hope.

GALATIANS 5:5 AMPC

Renewal

So each generation should set its hope anew
on God, not forgetting his glorious miracles
and obeying his commands.
PSALM 78:7 NLT

Raising children to be godly has never been easy, but today's world is changing so quickly parents have the difficult job of keeping up. Most young adults, let alone children, have no concept of what it was like to grow up without the technology that gives us instant access to any kind of information or entertainment we could want. Setting up limits and enforcing them is more challenging every day.

But scripture says each generation is to make its own decision about God. In order to do so, children need to hear about God's miracles, His faithfulness in every situation. They need to learn the importance of obeying God's commands. And the only way they will is if their parents and other adults give testimony of what God has done and is doing in their lives. Our young people need to be exposed to the truths of scripture and the stories of God's working through the ages—from Creation through the events revealed in the book of Revelation. Most of all, this generation needs to see obedience to God's Word.

As the older generation, we must be in the Word ourselves to know what God requires of us, to be renewed daily, so we can correctly portray God before the younger generation. The responsibility rests on us.

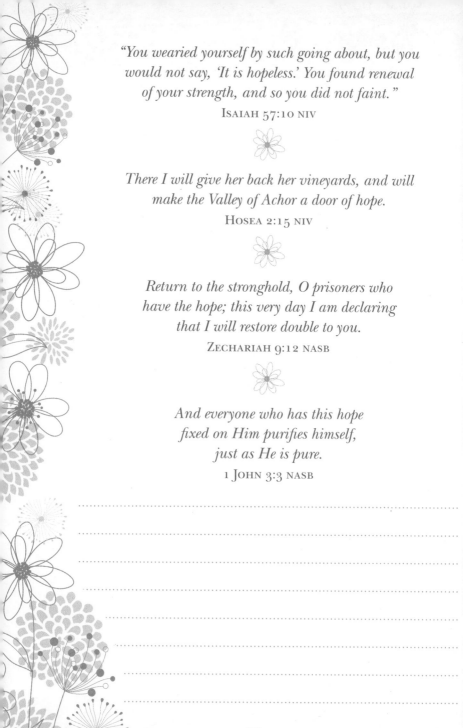

"You wearied yourself by such going about, but you would not say, 'It is hopeless.' You found renewal of your strength, and so you did not faint."

ISAIAH 57:10 NIV

There I will give her back her vineyards, and will make the Valley of Achor a door of hope.

HOSEA 2:15 NIV

Return to the stronghold, O prisoners who have the hope; this very day I am declaring that I will restore double to you.

ZECHARIAH 9:12 NASB

And everyone who has this hope fixed on Him purifies himself, just as He is pure.

1 JOHN 3:3 NASB

What oxygen is to the lungs,
such is hope to the meaning of life.
EMIL BRUNNER

By reading the scriptures I am so renewed that all
natures seem renewed around me and with me.
The sky seems to be a pure, a cooler blue, the trees
a deeper green. The whole world is charged with the
glory of God and I feel fire and music under my feet.
THOMAS MERTON

Expect to have hope rekindled. Expect your prayers
to be answered in wondrous ways. The dry seasons of
life do not last. The spring rains will come again.
SARAH BAN BREATHNACH

Cool Summer Shower

He will renew your life and
sustain you in your old age.
RUTH 4:15 NIV

Ruth's blessing of renewal is applicable to us today. *Renovatio* is Latin for "rebirth." It means casting off the old and embracing the new: a revival of spirit, a renovation of attitude. Something essential for women to espouse every day of their lives. Like a cool rain shower on a sizzling summer day, Ruth's hope was renewed by her Lord's touch, and ours will be too if we look to Him for daily replenishing.

Renewed Minds

Father, scripture tells us we must be renewed by the transformation of our minds. Our natural, sinful nature keeps us from desiring this until we accept Your gift of salvation. Knowing Christ and being in Your Word transforms our thinking, our actions, and our feelings. We are new creations, seeking to draw others to You. May our goal be as Paul's: to know You and the power of Your resurrection. Renew our minds today. Amen.

Against its will, all creation was subjected to
God's curse. But with eager hope, the creation
looks forward to the day when it will join God's
children in glorious freedom from death and decay.
ROMANS 8:20–21 NLT

But those who wait for the Lord [who expect, look for,
and hope in Him] shall change and renew their
strength and power; they shall lift their wings and
mount up [close to God] as eagles [mount up to
the sun]; they shall run and not be weary,
they shall walk and not faint or become tired.
ISAIAH 40:31 AMPC

The phoenix hope, can wing her way through
the desert skies, and still defying fortune's
spite; revive from ashes and rise.

MIGUEL DE CERVANTES SAAVEDRA

The day the Lord created
hope was probably the same
day he created Spring.

BERN WILLIAMS

Whenever I am tempted, whenever clouds arise,
When songs give place to sighing, when hope within me dies
I draw the closer to Him, from care He sets me free;
His eye is on the sparrow, and I know He watches me;
His eye is on the sparrow, and I know He watches me.

CIVILLA D. MARTIN

Divine Refreshment

You were tired out by the length of your road,
yet you did not say, "It is hopeless." You found
renewed strength, therefore you did not faint.
ISAIAH 57:10 NASB

By the end of each day, most women are ready to collapse. Tight schedules, relentless deadlines, and plaguing debts make our daily roads not just physically tiring but spiritually draining. Our reserves border on empty. How encouraging to know that renewed strength is available through the fountain that never runs dry. If we fill our buckets with living water—Bible reading, Christian music, inspirational books and DVDs—we will not faint, but enjoy divine refreshment.

Renewed Hope

Father, some days are just plain hard. On those days, it's difficult to get our minds to focus on the truths of Your Word. We fail You. We are tempted to give up, saying, "Life's too hard." On those days, remind us of Your love. Remind us of Your faithfulness in the past. Remind us of the hope we have in Christ that this present world is not our eternal reality. In Christ's name, amen.

Create in me a pure heart, O God,
and renew a steadfast spirit within me.

PSALM 51:10 NIV

Do not be conformed to this world (this age), [fashioned after and
adapted to its external, superficial customs], but be transformed
(changed) by the [entire] renewal of your mind [by its new ideals
and its new attitude], so that you may prove [for yourselves] what
is the good and acceptable and perfect will of God, even the thing
which is good and acceptable and perfect [in His sight for you].

ROMANS 12:2 AMPC

Resurrection

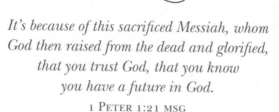

It's because of this sacrificed Messiah, whom
God then raised from the dead and glorified,
that you trust God, that you know
you have a future in God.

1 PETER 1:21 MSG

Christmas and Easter are two of the best-loved events on the church calendar. Have you ever pondered on the events surrounding Jesus' birth like Mary did? So much happened within a year's time: the angel's announcement, her cousin Elizabeth's late-in-life pregnancy, Joseph's near divorce until the angel revealed the truth of Mary's pregnancy, the journey to Bethlehem, her son's birth in a lowly stable, the angel's announcement to the shepherds, and later the wise men's visit and gifts.

Mary knew her son was the promised Messiah, but was she prepared to see Him cruelly nailed to the cross? Did she remember Anna's praise and Simeon's prophecy when she and Joseph took Jesus to the temple to present Him to the Lord?

Then she followed His public ministry that ended after three short years with an arrest, a mock trial, and crucifixion. What were her thoughts during the three days He was in the tomb? What joy and hope rose in her heart when the women returned with the news that Jesus was alive, resurrected from the dead!

Hallelujah! He is risen! He conquered death so that we might have life. Because of His resurrection we have a sure hope of a future with God.

"My brothers, I am a Pharisee, descended from Pharisees. I stand on trial because of the hope of the resurrection of the dead."

ACTS 23:6 NIV

Christ died for our sins, just as the Scriptures said. He was buried, and he was raised from the dead on the third day, just as the Scriptures said.

1 CORINTHIANS 15:3–4 NLT

Then we, the living ones who remain [on the earth], shall simultaneously be caught up along with [the resurrected dead] in the clouds to meet the Lord in the air; and so always (through the eternity of the eternities) we shall be with the Lord!

1 THESSALONIANS 4:17 AMPC

Christ the Lord is risen today, Alleluia!
Sons of men and angels say: Alleluia!
Raise your joys and triumphs high, Alleluia!
Sing, ye heavens and earth reply: Alleluia!

Lives again our glorious King, Alleluia!
Where, O death, is now thy sting? Alleluia!
Dying once He all doth save, Alleluia!
Where thy victory, O grave? Alleluia!

Soar we now where Christ has led, Alleluia!
Following our exalted Head, Alleluia!
Made like Him, like Him we rise, Alleluia!
Ours the cross, the grave, the skies, Alleluia!

CHARLES WESLEY

....

....

....

....

....

....

....

....

....

....

....

....

Hope Resurrected

*We had hoped that he would be the one
to set Israel free! But it has already been
three days since all this happened.*

LUKE 24:21 CEV

The scenario for this scripture is quite unusual. Two of Jesus' disciples are describing their lost hope due to the events surrounding Jesus' death to none other than Jesus Himself. They don't recognize Him as they walk together on the road to Emmaus after His resurrection. Spiritual cataracts blind them to the hope they thought was dead— right in front of them! Let's open our spiritual eyes to Jesus, who is walking beside us.

Rejoice!

Father, wow! Just thinking of Christ's perfect sacrifice on the cross and His resurrection lifts our spirits with joy and hope in the future. Without the resurrection we would have no hope, and as Paul said, we would be the most miserable of people. But we are not in despair. We serve a risen Savior. He's alive and with us today and every day. We rejoice in a hope that is eternal. Praise God!

"And I admit to living in hopeful anticipation that God will raise the dead, both the good and the bad. If that's my crime, my accusers are just as guilty as I am."

ACTS 24:15 MSG

Jesus said to her, I am [Myself] the Resurrection and the Life. Whoever believes in (adheres to, trusts in, and relies on) Me, although he may die, yet he shall live.

JOHN 11:25 AMPC

Therefore my heart rejoiced and my tongue exulted exceedingly; moreover, my flesh also will dwell in hope [will encamp, pitch its tent, and dwell in hope in anticipation of the resurrection].

ACTS 2:26 AMPC

Those who hope for no other
life are dead even for this.

JOHANN WOLFGANG VON GOETHE

I have suffered too much in this
world not to hope for another.

JEAN-JACQUES ROUSSEAU

We have always held to the hope,
the belief, the conviction that
there is a better life, a better
world, beyond the horizon.

FRANKLIN D. ROOSEVELT

Earth to earth, ashes to ashes, dust to dust; in sure and
certain hope of the Resurrection into eternal life.

BOOK OF COMMON PRAYER

....

....

....

....

....

....

....

....

That Morning

*You have placed your faith
and hope in God because he raised Christ
from the dead and gave him great glory.*

1 PETER 1:21 NLT

Have you ever wondered how Mary felt that Easter morning when she discovered Jesus' tomb empty? Already grieving, imagine the shock of discovering the body of her Savior—the One who held all her hopes and dreams—gone! How can that be? Maybe. . . ? Hope glimmers. But no—impossible. He did say something about resurrection, but that was figurative, wasn't it? Who are. . . You are? I must run and tell them. It's true! He has risen! He's alive! My hope lives too!

Our Redeemer Lives

Father God, we stand amazed in Your presence, wondering at the pure, unconditional, and vast love that caused You to send Your only Son to die for our sins. But You didn't leave Him in the grave. You raised Him up into new life, so that we might be raised with Him, alive in the hope of the Gospel. May our lives be a continual symphony of praise because He is our risen Lord. Amen.

"Now I am on trial because of my hope in the fulfillment of God's promise made to our ancestors. In fact, that is why the twelve tribes of Israel zealously worship God night and day, and they share the same hope I have. Yet, Your Majesty, they accuse me for having this hope!"
ACTS 26:6–7 NLT

*Christ died and rose again for this very purpose—
to be Lord both of the living and of the dead.*
ROMANS 14:9 NLT

For I know that my redeemer liveth.
JOB 19:25 KJV

Salvation

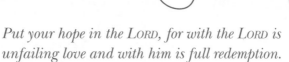

*Put your hope in the LORD, for with the LORD is
unfailing love and with him is full redemption.*

PSALM 130:7 NIV

Redemption is an amazing word—but one that in English doesn't begin to define all that is wrapped up in the Greek. In the ancient Roman and Greek societies, slavery was common. As the spoils of war, many slaves came to their masters as children. They knew no other way of life. The fortunate ones were bought by good masters, ones who treated them fairly yet expected good return for the purchase price. The not-so-fortunate found themselves in the slave market over and over. They knew the humiliation of being judged according to their size, their skills, or their beauty. Very few slaves had the guarantee they were bought never to be sold again.

That's one of the meanings of redemption—one that Paul stressed in his writing. Full redemption means the new owner paid the full price for a slave and then set the slave free, never to be sold again. That's what Jesus did when He paid our redemption price on the cross. He paid the ransom price our sin demanded, and redeemed us from the slave market of sin. . .never to be sold again. Whenever the accuser points out our sin, Christ stands before the Judge to show His wounded hands—proof that He paid the slave price— and claims us as His own. Hope placed in Jesus Christ is never disappointed. He has guaranteed our freedom forever.

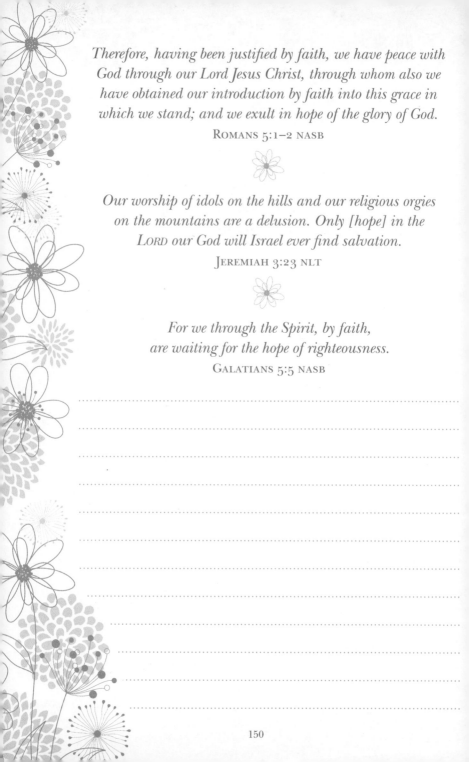

Therefore, having been justified by faith, we have peace with God through our Lord Jesus Christ, through whom also we have obtained our introduction by faith into this grace in which we stand; and we exult in hope of the glory of God.

ROMANS 5:1–2 NASB

Our worship of idols on the hills and our religious orgies on the mountains are a delusion. Only [hope] in the LORD our God will Israel ever find salvation.

JEREMIAH 3:23 NLT

For we through the Spirit, by faith, are waiting for the hope of righteousness.

GALATIANS 5:5 NASB

My hope is in the Lord
Who gave Himself for me,
And paid the price of
all my sin at Calvary.
For me He died,
For me He lives,
And everlasting life
and light He freely gives.
NORMAN J. CLAYTON

Our hope is in no
other save in Thee;
Our faith is built upon
Thy promise free;
Lord, give us peace,
and make us calm and sure,
That in Thy strength
we evermore endure.
"I Greet Thee, Who My Sure Redeemer Art"
JOHN CALVIN

Patience of Hope

*We call to mind your work of faith, your labor of love,
and your patience of hope in following our Master,
Jesus Christ, before God our Father.*

1 THESSALONIANS 1:3 MSG

Labor. The word alone draws a shudder from the most stalwart of pregnant women. Just as laboring to bring forth new physical life requires patience, birthing new spiritual life may require an intensive labor of love: ceaseless prayer. Countless mothers on their knees praying for the salvation of a loved one have rejoiced in answered prayer. Their secret? Patience of hope.

Amazing Love

Father God, what amazing love You demonstrated toward us! Because of Your holiness You cannot tolerate sin in Your presence. Long before You created the world, You had a relationship with us in mind. You knew Adam and Eve would fall, so You provided the solution. You would send Your Son into the world to pay the awful price demanded by sin. Because of Jesus' sacrifice and resurrection, we are now Your children, righteous and holy before You.

I am worn out waiting for your rescue,
but I have put my hope in your word.
PSALM 119:81 NLT

The LORD is good unto them that wait for him, to the
soul that seeketh him. It is good that a man should both
hope and quietly wait for the salvation of the LORD.
LAMENTATIONS 3:25–26 KJV

But as for me, I will look to the Lord and confident in Him
I will keep watch; I will wait with hope and expectancy
for the God of my salvation; my God will hear me.
MICAH 7:7 AMP

This is all my hope and peace,
Nothing but the blood of Jesus.
ROBERT LOWRY

I'm possessed of a hope that
is steadfast and sure,
Since Jesus came into my heart!
And no dark clouds of doubt
now my pathway obscure,
Since Jesus came into my heart!
RUFUS H. McDANIEL

Do a Little Dance

Then Miriam the prophet, Aaron's sister,
took a tambourine and led all the women as
they played their tambourines and danced.

EXODUS 15:20 NLT

Can you imagine the enormous celebration that broke out among the children of Israel when God miraculously saved them from Pharaoh's army at the Red Sea? Even dignified prophetess Miriam grabbed her tambourine and cut loose with her girlfriends. Despite adverse circumstances, she heard God's music and did His dance. Isn't that our goal today? To hear God's music above the world's cacophony and do His dance as we recognize everyday miracles in our lives?

Living Godly Lives

Precious Lord, we thank You for the presence of the Holy Spirit who teaches us how to live godly in this ungodly world. When we accept Your free gift of salvation, made possible through the sacrifice of Your Son, You give us everything we need to live godly lives. When we are weak, You give us power to overcome even the strongest of temptations. Words alone will never express our gratitude for such a gift. Amen.

My rightness and justice are near,
My salvation is going forth,
and My arms shall rule the peoples;
the islands shall wait for and expect Me,
and on My arm shall they trust
and wait with hope.
ISAIAH 51:5 AMPC

Remember your leaders. . .who brought to you the Word of God. . . .
Imitate their faith (their conviction that God exists and is. . .the
Provider and Bestower of eternal salvation through Christ, and their
leaning of the entire human personality on God in absolute trust
and confidence in His power, wisdom, and goodness).
HEBREWS 13:7 AMPC

Shelter

In You, O Lord, do I put my trust and seek refuge;
let me never be put to shame or [have my hope in You]
disappointed; deliver me in Your righteousness!

PSALM 31:1 AMPC

David's popularity with the people of Israel soon turned King Saul's favor away from him. Saul didn't know that David had been anointed king in his place. It may not have made any difference if he had known. But it mattered to David that Saul was anointed before him, and therefore he honored Saul and refused to kill the Lord's anointed, even when David feared for his life.

Many of David's psalms were written from his hiding places in the wilderness. When Saul's fury led him to attempt murdering David to rid himself of the nuisance, still David refused to retaliate.

Several times David's men urged him to kill Saul when offered the chance. But David was willing to wait on God's timing.

However, there were times when David wondered how much longer the chase could go on. He was tired of keeping one step ahead of Saul. David quickly learned that God was his only true refuge.

Today we still have the hope that God will shelter us from the storms of life. He is always faithful in providing a way of escape when the burdens get too heavy to bear. With God as our refuge we need never to lose our hope that the future belongs to Him. He will shelter us forever from our enemies.

Having hope will give you courage.
You will be protected and will rest in safety.
JOB 11:18 NLT

LORD, don't terrorize me! You alone
are my hope in the day of disaster.
JEREMIAH 17:17 NLT

Those who live in the shelter of the Most High will
find rest in the shadow of the Almighty. This I
declare about the LORD: He alone is my refuge,
my place of safety; he is my God, and I trust him.
PSALM 91:1–2 NLT

So trust him absolutely, people;
lay your lives on the line for him.
God is a safe place to be.
PSALM 62:8 MSG

Our God, our help in ages past,
Our hope for years to come,
Our shelter from the stormy blast,
And our eternal home.

Our God, our help in ages past,
Our hope for years to come,
Be Thou our guard
while troubles last,
And our eternal home.
ISAAC WATTS

In all things it is better to hope than to despair.
JOHANN WOLFGANG VON GOETHE

....

....

....

....

....

....

....

....

....

....

....

....

....

My Refuge

God is our refuge and strength,
always ready to help in times of trouble.
PSALM 46:1 NLT

What is your quiet place? The place you go to get away from the fray, to chill out, think, regroup, and gain perspective? Mine is a hammock nestled beneath a canopy of oaks in my backyard. . .nobody around but birds, squirrels, an occasional wasp, God, and me. There I can pour out my heart to my Lord, hear His comforting voice, and feel His strength refresh me. We all need a quiet place. God, our refuge, will meet us there.

Perfect Refuge

Lord God, You are our shelter, a solid rock, our fortress, our shield, and our strength. You shelter us under Your wings away from the heat of the day and the storm and rain. Your very presence shelters us safe from the enemy's reach. When You tuck us away in Your refuge, You promise us perfect peace because our minds are fixed on You. Quiet and secure. We praise You, Father.

The LORD is my solid rock, my fortress, my rescuer.
My God is my rock—I take refuge in him!—he's my
shield and my salvation's strength, my place of safety
and my shelter. My savior! Save me from violence!
2 SAMUEL 22:2–3 CEB

It will be a shelter and shade from the heat of the day,
and a refuge and hiding place from the storm and rain.
ISAIAH 4:6 NIV

"They are before the throne of God and serve him day
and night in his temple; and he who sits on the
throne will shelter them with his presence."
REVELATION 7:15 NIV

The Lord's our Rock, in Him we hide,
A Shelter in the time of storm;
Secure whatever ill betide,
A Shelter in the time of storm.

VERNON J. CHARLESWORTH

Be Thou my battle Shield,
Sword for the fight;
Be Thou my Dignity,
Thou my Delight;
Thou my soul's Shelter,
Thou my high Tower:
Raise Thou me heavenward,
O Power of my power.

DALLAN FORGAILL

Slathered in SPF

You are my refuge and my shield;
I have put my hope in your word.
PSALM 119:114 NIV

These days, the word shield evokes images of glistening sunbathers dotting beaches and carefree children slathered in sunscreen. Like the psalmist's metal shield, sunscreen deflects dangerous rays, preventing them from penetrating vulnerable skin—higher SPF for more protection. When we are immersed in God's Word, we erect a shield that deflects Satan's attempts to penetrate our weak flesh. Internalizing more of God's Word creates a higher SPF: Scripture Protection Factor. Are you well coated?

Protection

Father God, the battle is fierce, and we are weary. You promise to be our shield, our protection in the midst of the war. When our arms grow weak from exertion and we are unable to hold our own shields, You raise Your Word as a shield, deflecting every fiery dart the enemy showers on us. And when the battle is over, You take us into Your tower of refuge so we can recoup our strength. We love You.

*But you are a tower of refuge to the poor, O L*ORD*, a tower of refuge to the needy in distress. You are a refuge from the storm and a shelter from the heat. For the oppressive acts of ruthless people are like a storm beating against a wall.*

ISAIAH 25:4 NLT

*"As for God, His way is blameless; the word of the L*ORD *is tested; He is a shield to all who take refuge in Him."*

2 SAMUEL 22:31 NASB

*I have taken my refuge in you, my L*ORD *God, so I can talk all about your works!*

PSALM 73:28 CEB

Spiritual Growth

I pray that your hearts will be flooded with
light so that you can understand the confident
hope he has given to those he called—his holy people
who are his rich and glorious inheritance.

EPHESIANS 1:18 NLT

Looking at family photos and videos of past events is so much fun. We marvel at how quickly time has passed and how quickly things and people have changed. The trees in the yard were once small but now are tall and strong. The home we live in has been remodeled to fit the needs of a growing family. But when those pictures were taken, time seemed to stand still. It was hard to imagine a future time when everything was older.

It's good to take time and reflect on the past because it is only from that perspective that we can measure growth.

Many of us use the first of a new year or a birthday to think back, see where we've been successful, where we've failed or stagnated, and then make goals for growth in the future. Others do it monthly or weekly, though it is hard to see growth in those shorter periods of time.

When we ask, the Lord often puts the strong light of His Word on the particular area of growth we want to examine. In that light there is no shadow; everything is exposed, the good and the bad. And we see more clearly the hope that lights our pathway and keeps us moving forward, confident in our Savior and Lord.

*We're not barging in on the rightful work of others,
interfering with their ministries, demanding a place in the
sun with them. What we're hoping for is that as your lives
grow in faith, you'll play a part within our expanding work.*

2 CORINTHIANS 10:15 MSG

*But grow in the grace and knowledge of our Lord
and Savior Jesus Christ. To Him be the glory,
both now and to the day of eternity. Amen.*

2 PETER 3:18 NASB

*The righteous shall flourish like the palm tree:
he shall grow like a cedar in Lebanon.*

PSALM 92:12 KJV

Make no little plans; they have no magic to stir men's blood. . . . Make big plans; aim high in hope and work.
DANIEL H. BURNHAM

Hope unbelieved is always considered nonsense. But hope believed is history in the process of being changed.
JIM WALLIS

....
....
....
....
....
....
....
....
....
....
....
....
....
....
....
....

Working Out

I will never give up hope or stop praising you.
PSALM 71:14 CEV

Praise is like a muscle; if we don't exercise it regularly, it becomes weak and atrophied. But if we flex and extend an attitude of gratitude daily, praise grows into a strong, dependable force that nurtures hope and carries us through the worst of circumstances. Like Helen Keller, though blind and deaf, we'll praise our Creator: "I thank God for my handicaps, for through them, I have found myself, my work, and my God."

No Standing Still

Father, for a believer there are no times of stagnation. We're either moving forward closer to Jesus or we are slipping away. It is hard work, but for most of us, we desire a close, intimate relationship with Jesus, our Savior. Knowing Him means we know You. Open our eyes of understanding to see where we may be slipping. Enlighten our minds to turn toward You and Your Word. Amen.

So come on, let's leave the preschool fingerpainting exercises on Christ and get on with the grand work of art. Grow up in Christ. The basic foundational truths are in place.
HEBREWS 6:1 MSG

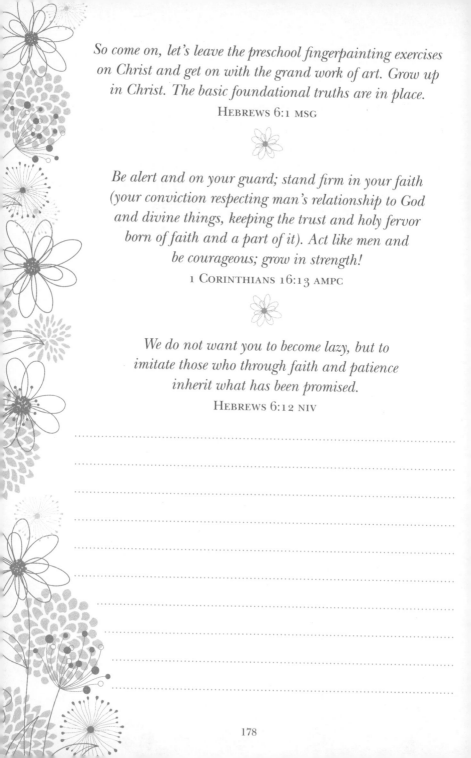

Be alert and on your guard; stand firm in your faith (your conviction respecting man's relationship to God and divine things, keeping the trust and holy fervor born of faith and a part of it). Act like men and be courageous; grow in strength!
1 CORINTHIANS 16:13 AMPC

We do not want you to become lazy, but to imitate those who through faith and patience inherit what has been promised.
HEBREWS 6:12 NIV

Never stop believing in dreaming, and never stop
dreaming of believing. That is what gives us
hope, and what keeps us alive.

UNKNOWN

Hope is the companion of power, and mother
of success; for who so hopes strongly has
within him the gift of miracles.

SAMUEL SMILES

At first people refuse to believe that a strange new thing
can be done, then they begin to hope it can be done,
then they see it can be done—then it is done and all the
world wonders why it was not done centuries ago.

FRANCES BURNETT

....

....

....

....

....

....

....

....

....

....

New Life

God is so good, and by raising Jesus from death,
he has given us new life and a hope that lives on.
1 PETER 1:3 CEV

The words of a song I wrote while pregnant with my first child exult in the similarities between new physical life and new spiritual life in Christ: "New life stirs within me now. Like a soft breeze, transforming me now. It's a miracle of love, precious blessing from above. My heart has taken wings. . .lift me up!" New life. By the goodness of God, we can experience this precious transformation no less miraculous than a baby growing within us.

Renewed Hope

Lord God, as our faith grows so does our love for You. As our love increases so does our desire to be like Christ. Hope is renewed, and our steps take us forward with renewed purpose. We begin to see the plan You have for us, not for evil but for hope and a future. Open our spiritual eyes to see Your blessings each day. We love You. In Christ's name, amen.

We do not boast therefore, beyond our proper limit, over other men's labors, but we have the hope and confident expectation that as your faith continues to grow, our field among you may be greatly enlarged, still within the limits of our commission.
2 CORINTHIANS 10:15 AMPC

Epaphras. . .[is] always striving for you earnestly in his prayers, [pleading] that you may [as persons of ripe character and clear conviction] stand firm and mature [in spiritual growth], convinced and fully assured in everything willed by God.
COLOSSIANS 4:12 AMPC

Strength

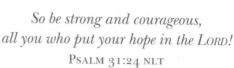

So be strong and courageous,
all you who put your hope in the LORD!
PSALM 31:24 NLT

In the first two chapters of Luke we are introduced to two boys at their births. One was born to an older couple who had never been able to have a child before. An angel announced his birth to his father who served in the temple as a priest. When the father expressed disbelief in what the angel told him, he was struck dumb until the promised boy was born and his name was revealed. His name was John, and he was the forerunner of the Messiah, the voice who cried out of the wilderness. In Luke 1:80, we are told "the child continued to grow and to become strong in spirit" (NASB).

An angel announced the impending conception of the second boy to a virgin who was betrothed to be married. Soon after, the young mother went to visit her older cousin who was also unexpectedly pregnant. The older woman confirmed the younger was the chosen mother of the promised Messiah. Later, at the urging of the angel, Joseph married Mary and Jesus was born. Luke tells us that this "Child continued to grow and become strong, increasing in wisdom" (2:40 NASB).

God caused both boys to become strong and increase in the skills they would need for their earthly ministries. For all who hope in God, He makes strong, each according to the purpose for which He made us.

....

....

....

Pardon for sin and a peace that endureth,
Thy own dear presence to cheer and to guide;
Strength for today and bright hope for tomorrow,
Blessing all mine, with ten thousand beside!

THOMAS CHISHOLM

A key to strengthening spiritual muscles
and enduring hardship is finding
strength in the Word of God.

WALTER MARTIN

God's Purpose

Father, You have a purpose for each of Your children. While You may not always reveal it to us, You always work within Your plan, orchestrating events and people who will influence us to follow You with whole hearts. You equip us and make us strong in the places where He needs us. Sustain us with the hope that is ours because of Jesus. We love You. Amen.

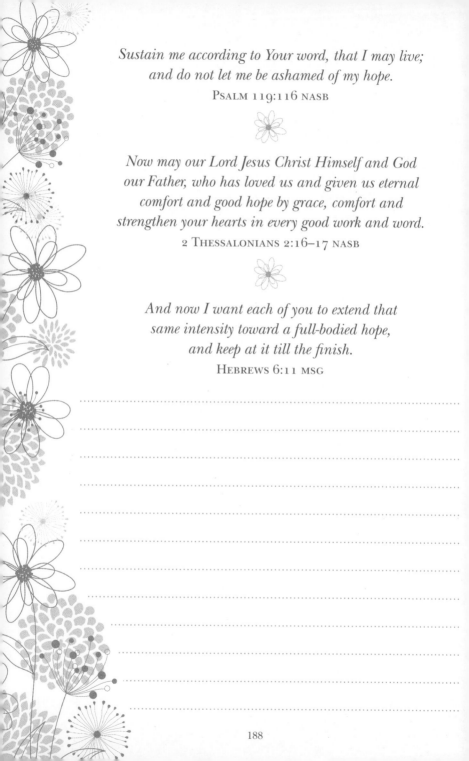

Sustain me according to Your word, that I may live;
and do not let me be ashamed of my hope.
PSALM 119:116 NASB

Now may our Lord Jesus Christ Himself and God
our Father, who has loved us and given us eternal
comfort and good hope by grace, comfort and
strengthen your hearts in every good work and word.
2 THESSALONIANS 2:16–17 NASB

And now I want each of you to extend that
same intensity toward a full-bodied hope,
and keep at it till the finish.
HEBREWS 6:11 MSG

I place no hope in my strength, nor in my works;
but all my confidence is in God my protector,
who never abandons those who have put
all their hope and thought in him.

FRANCOIS RABELAIS

Like strength is felt from
hope and despair.

ALEXANDER POPE

Each time a man stands for an ideal, or acts to
improve the lot of others, or strikes out against
injustice, he sends a tiny ripple of hope, and
crossing each other from a million different
centers of energy and daring, those ripples
build a current which can sweep down the
mightiest walls of oppression and resistance.

ROBERT FRANCIS KENNEDY

Designer Label

We wish that each of you would always be eager to show how strong and lasting your hope really is.
HEBREWS 6:11 CEV

Our behavior is always on display, and like it or not, we are judged by our actions. . .and inactions. Without an explanation for our behavior—that we're motivated by faith to be Christlike—people will make up their own ideas: Her mama taught her right; she was just born nice; she acts sweet so everyone will like her. Isn't it better to be up-front and give credit to the One we're emulating? Wear the label of your Designer proudly.

Hope and Strength

Father, You are the hope and strength of Your people. Jesus said that without Him we could do nothing. Oh, we attempt to do it on our own, but we always fail. In Your lovingkindness, You pick us up, brush us off, and gently rebuke our futile efforts to accomplish Your purpose without You. Your love and Your patience are inexhaustible. You alone deserve all the praise and glory for the hope that lies within us. Amen.

The Lord also shall roar out of Zion,
and utter his voice from Jerusalem;
and the heavens and the earth shall shake:
but the Lord will be the hope of his people,
and the strength of the children of Israel.

Joel 3:16 kjv